Ernest Forbes has written comedy for stage, books, radio and television including material for Dave Allen, Les Dawson, Roy Hudd and The Two Ronnies

He is a high handicap golfer as that is the state in which he normally plays.

ERNEST FORBES

THE GOLFER'S GAG BAG

A Futura Book

Copyright ©Ernest Forbes 1986

First published in Great Britain in 1986
by Futura Publications, a Division of
Macdonald & Co (Publishers) Ltd
London & Sydney

ISBN 0 7088 3021 8

Photoset in North Wales by
Derek Doyle & Associates, Mold, Clwyd
Cartoons by Clare Harper
Printed and bound in Great Britain by
Cox & Wyman Ltd, Reading

Futura Publications
A Division of
Macdonald & Co (Publishers) Ltd
Greater London House
Hampstead Road
London NW1 7QX

A BPCC plc Company

GOLFING DEFINITIONS

(Not to be found in The Golfers' Guide)

BALL:	An inanimate object with a will of its own.
BIRDIE:	What you get under the mistletoe.
BOGEY:	Never did say 'Play it again Sam!'
BUNKER:	Hitler's last known residence.
CADDIE:	The poor chap who is always left holding the bag.
CHIP:	Can be purchased at a Chinese carry-out.
CUP:	Always appears to be smaller when you're putting.
DIVOT:	U.F.O.
FAIRWAY:	'... fields always seem greener.'
GOLF:	Eighteen spells of anger and frustration combined with bouts of very poor arithmetic.
GOLFER:	One who shouts fore, takes seven and puts down five.
GREENS:	Children should eat plenty of them.
HOLE:	Where the ball should be but isn't!

HOLE-IN-ONE: As in socks.

LIE: What you tell about your golfing ability when with non-golfers.

PAR: When you score below it it's skill, when your opponent does it's luck!

SHAFTS: Angie Dickinson has the best pair in Hollywood.

SCRATCH
  GOLFER: One who is itching to play.

TEE: The only thing to have if you're going to drive!

Oscar Wilde had his own views on golf. Here are some of his alleged comments:

'A harmless little sphere chased by men too old to chase anything else.'

* * *

'A man swinging a stick on which there is a better head than he has on his shoulders.'

* * *

'A childish game played by adults who purposely hit a ball into the most inaccessible places so they can indulge in foul language when trying to recover it.'

* * *

'No I don't play golf. If I wished to put a ball in a hole I'd drop it in.'

* * *

'Golf is a game where there is a ball at one end of a stick and a fool at the other.'

* * *

'The first 18 holes have no part in a golfer's ruddy complexion which is caused by the time spent at the 19th hole.'

Many golf clubs claim their courses are safe from fire as to save the players from this danger sprinkler systems have been installed on the greens.

The perfect age for a lady golfer is 35 especially if she happens to be 50.

Eddie Mills had been hit on the head by a golf ball at the tenth and died immediately. He arrived at Heaven to be greeted by St. Peter.

St. Peter examined the records and nodded, 'Only one blemish. That was when you took the Lord's name in vain on a golf course last year. Now I am also a golfer so if you tell me what happened perhaps I could help.'

'Well,' said Eddie, 'to win the match I had to get a birdie at the last hole which was a par five. I sliced my first shot into the rough.'

'Was that when you took the Lord's name in vain?' asked St. Peter.

'Oh no, sir,' said Eddie. 'I played out of the rough without any bother but landed on the edge of a sand bunker and the ball almost stuck but then slowly rolled back into the soft sand.'

'So that was when you took the Lord's name in vain,' stated St. Peter.

'No not then. I'm rather good at bunker shots. I took careful aim, used the open stance and with a smooth shot landed ten inches from the flag.'

'You don't mean,' thundered St. Peter, 'you missed a bloody ten inch putt?'

Dean Martin had a side bet that he could hole in three at the tenth on the Hollywood Golf Course. His first shot went straight up the fairway but he badly hooked his second shot and landed in the rough seventy yards from the green.

'Now for one helluva putt,' said the singer.

'Good Heavens! I think old Smithers is having a stroke!'

'Just make sure he marks it on his card!'

It was all square at the 18th Hole and the game depended on a short putt by Charlie. Slowly he measured the distance, checked the green, tested the wind, had a couple of practice swings then prepared to putt. Just then on a nearby road a funeral passed and much to the surprise of his companions Charlie stepped back, removed his cap and stood very still until the funeral passed completely by then he played the shot and holed the ball.

His partner slapped him on the back and said, 'Well done Charlie, but why did you stop until the funeral passed? Was it someone very important?'

'Well,' replied Charlie, 'its just that if she had lived we would have been married twenty-five years to-day!'

Some golfers are very superstitious, always using the same putter or wearing the same cap. One such golfer always had the same caddie even though the caddie was continually troubled with hiccough. One day the man badly missed his drive and turning to the caddie snarled, 'That was your fault with your damned hiccough.'

'But I didn't hiccough,' defended the caddie.

'I know that,' replied the golfer, 'but I allowed for it.'

When David Steele was asked how he kept himself fit for golf when he was so busy he replied, 'Easy. I jog every day – twice around Cyril Smith.'

Boring Young Man: 'I'm a little stiff from golf.'
Pretty Young Girl: 'Oh? Is that far from here?'

Golf professional to lady pupil. 'Now the first thing you do is to address the ball.'
    Lady Pupil: 'Hello ball!'

The man strode into the house and snorted, 'Dr. Thompson says I can't play golf.'
    His wife asked anxiously, 'Did he see you at the hospital?'
    'No, on the golf course.'

First Wife: 'Does your husband play much golf each week?'

Second Wife: 'Oh thirty-six holes roughly speaking.

First Wife: 'And how many without bad language?'

The golfer was sentenced to be hanged.

'Do you mind,' he asked the hangman, 'if I take a couple of practice swings?'

Frankly I'm going to give up playing golf. It's got to the stage where I can't even win when I play on my own.

Sir Harry Lauder, the great Scots comedian was fond of a game of golf and a popular story is told about a round he had just finished at Gleneagles. As he left the course he said, 'Here's something for a glass of hot whiskey,' and pressed something into caddie's hand.

When the man opened his hand he found a lump of sugar.

Mark Jones approached the club professional and invited him for a drink in the clubhouse. When they were seated and sipping their drinks Jones leaned towards the professional and asked, 'Jack how long have I been with the club?'

'About ten years Mr. Jones,' replied the professional.

'So you've seen me play quite a lot.'

'I have indeed.'

'Well I know I can count on you for honest advice so tell me how I can cut about six strokes off my game.'

The professional thought for a moment before replying, 'I suggest you stop playing at the 17th hole!'

The Reverend Ian Paisley came home from a round of golf and threw his bag in the corner.

'How did it go dear?' asked his wife.

'Well I broke eighty-five,' replied the big man, 'and you know I can't afford to break eighty-five clubs at the price they are to-day!'

You can always tell widows in a Beverley Hills golf club. They play with black balls.

Scotsman: 'I lost a brand new ball this morning.'
Wife: 'What happened?'
Scotsman: 'The string broke.'

It is well known that golf has been the cause of more lying than an income tax form.

The trouble with my wife is that she stands too close to the ball – after she's hit it!'

Golf is like sex – you don't have to know anything about it to enjoy it.

The economy of the country is so bad since Margaret Thatcher took over that in some golf clubs you can't putt until the grazing sheep have been moved.

The Siamese walked up to the clubhouse and asked, 'Do you have a tee for two?'

Flynn noticed that before each shot Father Murphy muttered a short prayer.

At the 14th hole Flynn had a particularly long putt. He studied the lie and then said, 'Would a prayer do me any good Father?'

'No.'

'Why not?'

'Because you're a rotten putter!'

Errol Flynn and Freddie McAvoy were enjoying a mixed foursome with two very charming ladies.

At the 10th hole Errol Flynn missed a very short putt and exclaimed, 'Oh balls!' and, on seeing the shocked expressions of the two ladies continued quickly, '-picnics, and parties are things I remember with great pleasure.'

Reginald was seated next to a beautiful redhead at a dinner party. Throughout the meal he told her of all his achievements as a golfer and the girl listened politely with an occasional 'My goodness.'

As they sipped their coffee Reginald said, 'I'm

afraid I've been monopolizing the conversation and talking nothing but golf.'

'Oh that's alright,' said the girl. 'But what is golf?'

'I don't know if God exists,' said a golf club secretary, 'but with what's going on in our clubhouse it would be better for His reputation if He didn't.'

The Two men were slowed by the two ladies playing before them. The two ladies were not only slow playing but would also stand chatting at each green. At last one man got so fed up he exclaimed, 'I'm going to tell them to get a move on!'

While his friend went to speak to the ladies the other man settled himself comfortably on the bank. However, he was no sooner settled than his friend rushed back and threw himself down behind the bank.

'Phew!' gasped the breathless golfer. 'That was a close call.'

'What happened?' asked his friend.

'Well, as I got near I realised one was my wife and the other my mistress so I got back before they saw me. Means I can't move until they go.'

'Don't worry,' said the other golfer. 'I'll go and hurry them on.'

So saying the golfer left the bank only to scramble back a moment later looking very flustered. 'Small world, isn't it?' he spluttered.

First Girl: 'The club professional says I play a lot like Nancy.'

Second Girl: 'Lopez or Sinatra?'

Reason for playing through:

'My house is on fire.'

'Been told my wife has had an accident and has been rushed to hospital.'

'Heard on the radio the world is coming to an end any moment.'

'My mother-in-law is trapped in a lift.'

'My car has just been stolen.'
'My boss is playing behind me.'

'What club should I use?' asked the lady golfer?
'Lady, the way you play,' replied the caddie, 'it really doesn't matter.'

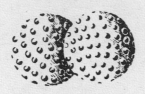

'Your first day on the course? How did you do?'
'I shot seventy.'
'Wonderful!'
'And to-morrow I play the second hole!'

After a really terrible shot the beginner had removed a huge divot and looked helplessly at the caddie. 'What should I do?'

'Well if you can get that divot home, plant daffodils in it!'

'It's a dirty lie!' exclaimed Thompson when he was told his ball had landed in the middle of a mud hole.

Wife: 'I know it's too much to expect, but if you ever spend a Saturday with me instead of playing golf I think I'd drop dead.'
Husband: 'It'll do you no good trying to bribe me.'

Leslie: 'I play golf every day to keep fit.'
Nora: 'Fit for what?'
Leslie: 'More golf.'

Mick was keeping an eye on his opponent, Patrick, who was in the rough.

When Patrick returned to the fairway Mick asked, 'How many – three?'

'No just two,' answered Patrick.

'I saw three.'

'One was a practice swing.'

'Shure now, it's the first time I've ever heard anyone curse after a practice swing.'

If you tell an untruth about your score don't try to better it or you may get a one stroke penalty for improving your lie.

At the World Golfers' Convention Angie Dickinson was voted the lady with whom they would most like to play a round.

Dean Martin once said of Angie Dickinson 'I don't know if she plays golf but she sure has a great set of shafts!'

'What do you mean you practice golf all winter?'
'Well I walk four miles to work every morning ... swing my umbrella every two hundred yards ... swear at my secretary ... stamp on the carpet ... then have a couple of drinks before going home!'

Murphy drove off powerfully and the ball went straight into a lake.
'Boy!' exclaimed Kelly. 'You drive just about as well as Teddy Kennedy!'

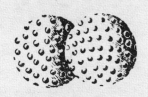

Billy Beggs was about to tee off at the 17th.

'I want a really good shot here,' he said. 'My mother-in-law is watching from behind the green.'

'Don't be daft,' said his partner. 'You couldn't possibly hit her, it's 400 yards at least.'

Stan was looking for his lucky golf socks.

'What are they like?' asked his wife.

'You'll easily spot them,' said Stan. 'There's a hole in one.'

Paddy always used the wrong club but always had the right answers.

'Shure if you tee off with your putter it will sometimes go further than if you miss it with your driver!'

As Mike O'Toole was being buried, some of his old clubmates stood around the grave, mourning their pal. A chilly wind and heavy rain only added to their misery. However, one man remarked cheerfully,

'Ah well, Mike wouldn't have played on a day like this anyway.'

Golfer: 'This is a water shot. Give me an old ball.'
Caddie: 'Sorry sir, but you've never had a ball long enough for it to get old.'

The telephone rang in the clubhouse.
'Is my husband there?' asked a woman.
'No madam.'
'How do you know when I haven't told you his name yet?'
'Madam, a husband is never here when a woman telephones. Club rule no. 67.'

'Is that my pal in the bunker?'
  'Or did that bastard get onto the green?'

Flannigan and O'Keefe were on the 1st tee. Flannigan took a big swing and got an unbelievable hole-in-one.

  'Bet you can't do that again,' said O'Keefe.
  'How much?'
  '£10.'
  'One condition.'
  'What's that?'
  'This time,' said Flannigan, 'I get to keep my eyes open!'

'I've been taking golf lessons,' said McDowell, after badly hooking a ball.
  'How many have you taken?' asked Kidd.
  'Twelve. Cost me £60.'
  'That's rough. You should see my brother.'
  'Is he a golf professional?'
  'No a solicitor. He'll help you get your money back!'

Collins and his caddie disagreed about which club to use at a short hole. Instead of taking the 3 iron the caddie suggested Collins selected his driver and played the ball. He sliced it sharply and it hit a tree to bounce off to strike a spectator on the head after which it rolled gently onto the green and trickled gently into the hole.

'See,' said Collins. 'I told you that was the right club.'

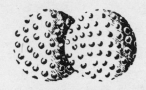

The best way to meet people at a golf club is to pick up the wrong ball.

'I'm sorry,' said the dentist into the telephone, 'but I couldn't give you an appointment this afternoon I have eighteen cavities to fill.' Then he replaced the received lifted his golf bag and headed for the golf course.

Husband: 'Your driving is improving darling you got so near the ball that time it trembled.'

There is a story in cricket circles that Mike Brearley, David Gower, Bob Willis and Derek Randall were playing a foursome in Australia. Mike Brearley teed off with a mighty whack and sent the ball sky high. Derek Randall immediately took off and circled underneath it shouting, 'I've got it, it's mine!'

It was Sunday morning at Royal Portrush and a number of foursomes were waiting to tee off. A Southern Irishman, who looked like Terry Wogan and had never played the course teed up. He stared reflectively at the ball then slowly walked over to the waiting golfers: 'This course is exactly two inches lower than the one I'm used to playing on.'

The way my doctor plays golf I think he must have given up his practice.

The wife was not happy about her husband leaving her to play golf every week-end and so she took up bowls.

'How did it go?' asked her husband when she returned after her first game.

'Well, at least I didn't lose any balls,' she replied triumphantly.

A rather chubby golfer was studying the Weight/-Height Chart at the scales in the locker room.

'What's the matter, Foster?' chided one of his companions. 'A little overweight?'

'Not at all,' replied Foster cheerfully. 'My weight's just fine, except according to this chart I should be ten inches taller.'

The lady swung time and time again but failed to make contact with the ball much to the amusement of her caddie.

'If you laugh at me again I'll hit you over the head with this club.'

'Maybe you could do that,' admitted the caddie. 'It's much bigger than the ball.'

'As a new member, how do you like the greens?'

'Lovely family.'

It was Saturday and Leslie was sitting watching television. His wife came into the room and said, 'Darling I thought you were playing golf to-day with Ken.'

'Certainly not. Would you play golf with a man who lies, cheats and moves his ball?'

'Indeed not!'

'Neither will Ken.'

Dolly Parton approached the club secretary and said, 'I'd like to join your club.'

'No problem at all,' beamed the secretary – twice.

'What equipment do I need?'

'None. I think you have it all,' replied the secretary.

And there is no truth in the rumour that Dolly Parton plays off a pair rather than a par.

And as the Irishman said when he saw Dolly Parton playing golf, 'That's the best 'par' in the club.

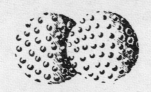

The club professional was approached by two women.

'Do you want to learn to play golf madam?' he asked one.

'Oh no,' she said. 'It's my friend here who wants to learn. I learned yesterday.'

He was lecturing his son: 'You're just a hopeless, no good golfer. Are you going to spend the rest of your life tramping around the course?'

'No dad,' said the son. 'I was going to ask you to buy me a golf buggy.'

'Give me a new set of clubs, a wonderful golf course and Angie Dickinson as a partner and you can keep the clubs and the golf course.'

'And this man,' accused the prosecuting lawyer pointing to the defendant, 'beat his wife to death with a golf club.'

The judge leaned forward with great interest as he looked at the man in the dock, 'As a matter of interest which club did you use?'

It was probably the same judge who on being told a man had beaten his wife to death with a 5 iron asked 'How many strokes?'

Golfer: Noticed any improvement since last year?'
Caddie: 'Yes sir you've cleaned your clubs.'

English Golfer: 'Excuse me do you mind if I play through?'
American Golfer: 'What's the rush pal?'
English Golfer: 'Just got word my house is on fire.'

As he had led a very good and pure life when George died he went to heaven where he was greeted by St. Peter.

'Welcome,' boomed St. Peter, 'glad to have you and I'm sure you'll be very happy here.'

'I'm sure I will,' replied George, 'except I'll miss playing golf.'

'Not here you won't,' said St. Peter, 'we have wonderful courses here, greens as smooth as satin and daylight all the time. If you like we'll have a round now.'

George found that the greens were as smooth as satin but there were also some very rough spots and approaching the 8th he saw a very stately figure standing knee deep in grass in such a spot. Much to George's surprise the golfer selected a wood to play out and George turned to St. Peter and remarked 'A wood to play out of that? Who does he think he is – God?'

'As a matter of fact that is God but he thinks he's Jack Nicklaus.'

'I've just hit a hole in one!' yelled the golfer jumping in glee.

'Oh isn't that nice,' replied his wife. 'Do it again dear I didn't see it.'

During instruction the club professional had a habit of taking his cap off, staring into it and then continue teaching. The pupils wondered why he did this until one day one of the class managed to look into the cap to find a piece of paper cellotaped inside on which was written 'A hook shot goes left, a slice goes right.'

They were seated around the television set watching the British Open.

'Turn it up a little,' said Bob.

'Ssh ...' whispered David, 'not while Player is putting.'

'Does he think of golf all the time?'

'No, but when he thinks, he thinks of golf.'

After much searching the caddie found a ball in the rough and handed it to the lady golfer who immediately disowned it.

'This is an old ball and mine was a new one,' she said.

'Yes miss,' said the caddie, 'but don't forget it's a long time since we started out.'

'The only good thing about golf is the 19th hole.' – W.C. Fields.

W.C. Fields was not a good golfer and normally had to be bribed to go on the course. In one match he was really getting the worst of it but he kept his temper (not an easy thing for Mr. Fields to do), however, when his opponent sliced a ball he exclaimed loudly, 'Ah my good fellow, I'm afraid you've landed in the bunker, I hope!'

A golfer should always be completely sober when explaining how he got a hole in one.

There is a story told that the Rev. Ian Paisley called at the home of one of his parishioners and as the husband was out he spoke to the wife.

'I have heard that John is in the habit of going to the golf club on the Sabbath.'

'Oh, but he doesn't play. He only goes over for a few drinks and a game of cards,' said the wife helpfully.

Rodney was hacking around in the rough for quite some time before the ball appeared.

'I say Rodney old boy, how many strokes did it take you to get out?' asked Cecil.

'One,' came the reply.

'But I counted seventeen.'

'Not at all,' said Rodney cooly, 'I took sixteen to kill a snake.'

'My husband is very outspoken, calls a spade a spade.'

'So does mine, but you want to hear what he calls his golf clubs.'

A girl went to the doctor to ask what she could do to prevent pregnancy.

'Play golf,' advised the doctor.

'Before or after?' she asked.

'Instead,' he replied.

The Rev. Ian Paisley is against sport of any kind being played on Sunday and it seems he didn't approve of ladies playing golf at all when he heard the object of the game was to go round the course in as little as possible!

When President Nixon resigned he had more time for his golf, which improved considerably so he couldn't understand why more people were beating him.

To me golf is an expensive way to play marbles.

Flynn and Kelly had been hitting the bottle before playing in the club championship and as Flynn was about to tee off he staggered over to Kelly and whispered, 'I can see three balls.'

'Well hit the middle one,' advised Kelly.

Flynn again took his stance, took a mighty swing, missed the ball and landed on his back.

'What's the matter?' asked Kelly. 'Didn't I tell you to hit the middle ball?'

'Yes but you didn't tell me to use the middle club,' replied Flynn.

The golfer was rather pleased with his drive and as he gazed up the fairway remarked, 'I wonder how many good golfers there are in this club.'

'One less than you think,' retorted his partner.

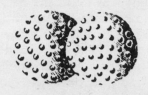

The foreman apologised for the bad language of one of his workman who had dropped a hammer on his foot.

'Not to worry,' said the housewife, 'I'm used to much worse. My husband and I play mixed foursomes.'

She was a golf widow and wasn't too happy about the situation so she took her husband's business associate Peter Butler as a lover.

One afternoon, when she and her lover were in bed her husband telephoned.

'I'll be home late to-night darling as we're playing an extra nine holes.'

'Oh that's alright dear,' said the wife. With whom are you playing?'

'My business associate, Peter Butler.'

When Harold Wilson was Prime Minister he was invited to open a new golf course. The ball was placed on a gold coloured tee and Mr Wilson was handed a brand new club. He positioned himself then took a mighty swing at the ball only to bury the head of the club into the ground about a foot behind the ball and lifting out a very large divot. Looking at the crater he then turned to the crowd and said in a solemn voice, 'Gentlemen, I declare this course well and truly opened!'

Another story of W.C. Fields is that a pretty young starlet was hired to get Fields to play golf and when he refused she pouted and said, 'Oh dear, then I don't know what to do with my week-end.'

'My dear lady,' growled Fields, 'why not put your hat on it!'

It was a dreadful day at Royal Portrush as the couple battled against the weather. 'Tell me again John,' said the shivering Josie, 'how much fun we're having, I keep forgetting.'

'Shame about Steele's wife.'

'What happened?'

'Steele was practicing with a 5 iron in his back garden, knocked the ball through the window and killed his wife.

'Well would you believe that? I have trouble with my 5 iron too!'

A golfing minister was asked by his wife why he would never let her play golf with him.

'My dear,' he replied, 'there are three things one should do in silence – ponder, pray and putt!'

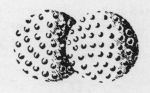

At an Irish Golf Club a visitor complained to the secretary about the long muddy drive to the clubhouse.

'Well,' said the secretary after a moment of reflection, 'if it was any shorter it wouldn't reach the clubhouse, would it?'

The caddie had carried clubs for Denis Compton in the morning and was telling his afternoon customer exactly how Denis Compton had played every shot, much to the annoyance of the golfer.

'Denis took a 9 iron for this one,' said the caddie.

'Well give me the 5,' growled the golfer.

At the next hole it was, 'Denis took a 4 iron here.'

When they reached the pond hole the caddie was silent.

'Don't stop now,' said the golfer. 'What did Denis Compton use here?'

'Well if he had been you he would have used an old ball,' came the reply.

They searched the rough for the ball and finally the lady golfer turned to her caddie and snapped, 'Why didn't you watch where the ball went?'

'I'm sorry, but it usually doesn't go anywhere. You took me by surprise!'

Now you can buy a golfer's computer. Every time you hit the total key it automatically subtracts 2.

The chimney sweep was watching the club's professional practising a few swings. The pro shouted to the sweep, 'Do you fancy a round?'

'Love to,' replied the sweep.

'Well hold on and I'll get you some clubs.'

'Don't bother,' said the sweep, 'I'll use my chimney rods.'

And so he did, selecting a rod as carefully as the professional selected a club. The sweep won by three strokes.

'You're quite a golfer,' said the professional. 'What's your handicap?'

'Electric fires,' was the curt reply.

McTavish had played on the same golf course for thirty years when he suddenly announced he was giving up golf.

His companions were astounded and wanted to know why.

'I've lost ma ball,' was the reply.

Another story about a golfer in Scotland. McNabb had been playing golf for twenty-five years with the same ball. One day he lost it and went to buy a new one.

He walked into the pro shop and announced, 'Well here I am again!'

Husky Young Golfer: 'First tee the ball.'
Pretty Young Girl: 'I tee it. What cwub do I use?'

The two drunken golfers had reached the 8th hole.

'Lishen,' slurred one, 'if you don't stop cheating I won't play with you ever again.'

'Cheating? Whaddya mean cheating? I'm not cheating.'

'Then who's tilting the green?'

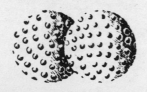

'I wish my wife would come back to me.'
    'She left you?'
    'I swapped her for Frank's putter.'
    'And now you miss her?'
    'No, but I could have swapped her for some new irons instead.'

'I played very badly to-day.'
    'Ah, your usual game!'

Greater love hath no man than he who gives up his golf for his wife.

If you try to teach your wife to play golf she can't hit a thing but teach her to drive a car and she never misses.

The angry golfer shook his fist at his caddie and shouted, 'If you laugh at me again I'll knock your head off!'

The caddie laughed, 'You wouldn't know which club to use!'

'Hello,' said George lifting the receiver.

'George, it's Harry. I've got it made. My wife's away for the day – let's have eighteen holes.'

'Sorry old chap so have I. My wife's away too and I have to look after the maid.'

The lady golfer had great difficulty hitting the ball much to the amusement of her caddie.

'I'm going to report you to the secretary as soon as we get back!' she snapped.

'All right, madam,' the caddie replied, 'but I've still got several hours before I need to worry.'

'What do you think would go well with my new yellow and red golf socks?'

'Wellington boots.'

A stranger joined a threesome on a public course at the 1st tee. 'What do you play?' he was asked.

'Seventy-seven,' he replied.

When they got to the 14th hole he picked up his ball and said, 'So long chaps. I've got my seventy-seven!'

Gordon Miller enjoyed life to the full. To the wine, women and song routine he also added golf. Alas, when the time came for Gordon to leave this world he went in a downwards direction and reported to the Devil at the gates of hell.

The Devil checked Gordon's record and said, 'You're in the right place. Which do you like most — the wine, the women, the song or the golf?'

'Why?' asked Gordon.

'We have them all here.'

'Oh the golf. It's a must.'

'Well follow me,' said the Devil and led him to a course more wonderful than he had ever dreamed of.

'Beautiful! Beautiful!' exclaimed Gordon. 'And they call this hell! May I have some clubs and balls, so I can play.'

'We haven't any,' replied the Devil.

'What?' cried Gordon. 'No clubs or balls with a fine course like this?'

'That's the hell of it,' grinned the Devil.

'Bending the elbow,' said the old hand, 'is the cause of wild swings and bad hooks. This is particularly true in the clubhouse bar!'

There is the story of the TV Stars Charity Match when Michael Parkinson hooked a ball which bounced into a girl's lap. She was sitting with the ball in her lap wondering what to do, when Parkinson approached her.

He assessed the situation, selected a wedge from

his bag and said, 'Brace yourself, ducky, this may smart a little.'

Jack and Tom were playing their usual Saturday morning round. Tom was playing his second shot from the 5th and he hooked the ball which struck a tree and rebounded to strike him on the head. He fell and lay quite still. Jack immediately ran to his friend and to his horror realised that Tom had gone to the great clubhouse in the sky.

A few weeks after Tom's death Jack was at home when the telephone rang and his wife answered. She came hurrying into Jack and gasped, 'Only I know Tom is dead I'd say he's on the telephone.'

Jack lifted the receiver and immediately recognised Tom's voice. 'Tom! I thought you were dead.'

'Of course I'm dead but I'm calling you from Heaven.'

'I didn't know you could telephone from Heaven.'

'As long as you have the code for Earth there's no problem.'

'Well nice of you to call.'

'I had to call. I've some news for you. Some good news and some bad news. What do you want first?'

'Oh the good news.'

'Well it really is heaven here regarding golf. Beautiful courses, no waiting, new clubs any time you want them, plenty of new balls and the best of all you can't miss a putt because the holes expand as you play to them.'

'That sounds wonderful. Now what's the bad news?'

'You're playing with me at three o'clock on Saturday!'

I play golf for my health so the lower my score the better I feel, that's why I cheat.

'Son why don't you take up golf and stop chasing around?'

'Well dad, I don't want to start chasing a golf ball until I'm too old to chase anything else.'

Jones had just finished with a score over 100. He turned to his caddie and said, 'I'll never be able to hold my head up again.'

'Oh I don't know sir,' was the reply. 'You've been doing it all afternoon.'

The club bore had cornered a non-playing member and had talked for two hours about the game he had just won. 'However, enough talk about me. Let's talk about you. What did you think about my twenty foot putt at the tenth?'

First Golfer: 'If those two women don't keep quiet, they'll drive me mad.'

Second Golfer: 'That wouldn't be a drive – more like a short putt.'

Dean Martin was not playing his usual good game and had just sliced a ball into the trees.

'Hell Dean, are you sober?' snorted his partner, a well known film producer.

'Occasionally,' smiled the star.

It was also W.C. Fields who remarked, 'Golf is like sex – you don't know how wonderful it is until you've tried it!'

Adam: 'I'm going to play a round.'
Eve: 'With whom?'

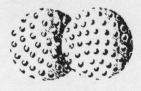

Golf Duffer: 'How can I improve my driving?'
Golf Pro: 'Have a police car follow you.'

An Irish golfer who tipped the scales at 20 stone was told to lose 7 stone immediately so he drank whiskey because it made his head light.

It is not generally known that Cyril Smith is a good golfer. He can putt and drive like a champion. In fact he can do anything except bend over and put the ball on the tee.

The only time a golfer tells the truth is when he calls another golfer a liar.

Clancey needed to sink a two foot putt to win the Captain's Prize. He was very nervous and studied the ground for about ten minutes, then fluttered a handkerchief to determine the exact direction of the wind. Finally he turned to his caddie and asked, 'How should I play this?'

'Keep it low,' grunted the caddie.

After playing the 1st hole the lady golfer turned to her caddie and asked, 'How many strokes?'

'I don't know,' replied the caddie.

'You're a caddie and you don't know how many strokes I took?'

'Madam, it's not a caddie you need, it's an accountant.'

'I never liked playing golf with my cabinet ministers,' recalled Sir Harold Wilson. 'Every time I shouted "Fore!" they all sang "He's a jolly good fellow!"'

The secretary of a Los Angeles golf club once confronted W.C. Fields with, 'Every time I see you on the course you have a bottle in your hand.'

'You don't expect me to keep it in my mouth all the time, do you?' retorted Fields.

Golfer: 'I've never played so badly before.'
Caddie: 'You mean to say you've played before?'

My wife is so overweight that when she puts the ball where she can see it she can't hit it and when she puts it where she can hit it she can't see it!

'How about that shot caddie? Could Tony Jacklin have played out like that?'

'Tony Jacklin would never have played in!'

Mike Brearley, the English cricket captain, shook his head sadly as he watched Derek Randall tee off at the sixth. 'The way Derek plays golf you would think he was batting in a limited over cricket match.'

Husband: 'Sorry I'm late dear, but we had a drinking contest after the game.'
Wife: 'Oh? And who came second?'

'Lost sir,' said the caddie.

'Another lost ball!' snorted the poor golfer.

'No sir, not the ball. We're lost.'

'Lost! We can't be lost. They told me you were the best caddie in the club.'

'I am sir. But we left the club twenty minutes ago!'

Golf is a game where if at first you don't succeed you try, try, try again. And, if you're honest, you mark it down on the scorecard.

Club Professional: 'Your trouble is that you don't address the ball properly.'
Angry Golfer: 'Dammit it man I've been polite long enough to the wretched thing.'

Steed was about to play a tricky shot on a public course when his talkive partner remarked, 'The traps on this course are very annoying, aren't they?'

'Yes,' replied Steed. 'So would you kindly shut yours!'

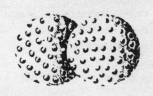

The two golfers were strangers to each other but they happened to come together one morning for a friendly round. One player, a minister of the church had five over par to reach the first hole only to miss a very short putt. He quietly put his putter into the bag without a murmur.

'By the way, what's your handicap?' asked his opponent.

'The Church,' was the gloomy reply.

The aged golfer had always said he wanted to die on the golf course and this is what happened one fine sunny day when he was playing a foursome, so his companions changed it to a threesome and carried him from hole to hole until they finished the game.

A rabbi and a priest were playing golf and the rabbi was soon eight strokes behind. It was his putting which was causing the trouble, no matter how easy the putt he simply couldn't sink the ball. Meanwhile his opponent had no trouble at all on the green. The rabbi noticed, however, that before putting the priest always blessed himself, so, as the situation was so serious the rabbi thought that he too would bless himself. At the next hole the rabbi had a comparatively easy putt nevertheless he blessed himself quickly played his shot and missed the hole.

'By the way,' smiled the priest, 'you have to be able to putt as well!'

Linda: 'I played golf to-day and I've got some good news and some bad news.'
Lee: 'What's the good news?'
Linda: 'I got a hole in one on the 1st green.'
Lee: 'And the bad news?'
Linda: 'I took 170 on the other 17.'

'I just don't know what's the matter,' complained David. 'But every year I seem to play worse golf than the year before.'

'How are you doing now?' asked Archie.

'Don't ask,' replied David. 'Already I'm playing next year's game.'

He: 'I played golf to-day and broke seventy.'
She: 'That's a lot of clubs to break.'

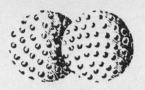

'The closest Michael Parkinson ever came to a hole-in-one was ten,' observed Jimmy Tarbuck.

He was the only person I knew who addressed the ball twice – before and after swinging.

The only trouble in playing golf with ex President Gerald Ford is the Secret Service. when you hit a ball the trees run along with you.

One golfer got so disgusted with the way he was playing he took his set of clubs and smashed every one into bits. He rushed into the clubhouse, grabbed a knife and slashed his wrists. A friend walked over and asked, 'How about a game to-morrow?' The man quickly held his wrists together to stop the bleeding and said, 'Good idea, what time?'

A new golfer was playing a short hole. With a full swing he gave the ball a mighty thump. The ball ricocheted off a tree, hit another tree, bounced off a rock and finally landed on the green about four inches from the hole. 'Dammit,' he said, 'if I had only hit it just a little harder!'

Bob Hope once remarked that golf was no longer a rich man's sport as there were too many poor players.

61

Bart and Bert were playing a course in the Swiss Alps. Bart played into the rough and when he re-appeared Bert asked 'How many?'
  'Four.'
  'I heard eight.'
  'Four were echoes.'

Barber: 'I've found a new lotion which will grow hair on a golf ball.'
Customer: 'Does it work.'
Barber: 'Yes but it makes putting hellish hard.'

Mike looked at the ball thoughtfully as he pondered, 'Wonder how I can prevent topping the ball when I swing?'
Pat: 'Try turning it upside down.'

The club secretary called the professional, 'A number of the members have complained to me that you drink too much. One member claims he saw you drinking two at a time.'

'Not true,' answered the professional. 'One was my drink and the other a provisional.'

Two professional snooker players were having a round of golf and one of them missed a short putt.

'Balls,' he muttered.

'Let's not talk shop,' said his partner.

The Reverend Ian Paisley stood over his putt for a long time.

'What's he doing – praying?' asked an opponent.

'He finished praying a long time ago,' his partner replied. 'Now he's waiting for an answer.'

The two golfers started to play after a heavy bout of drinking. On the first green a large dog lay between the ball of one of the players. Without hesitation the man played straight for it.

'Good heavens,' gasped his opponent, 'didn't you see the dog?'

'Yes,' came the reply, 'but I didn't think it was real.'

Philip was about to sink a short putt on the 9th green when suddenly a woman dressed in a bridal gown came running toward him.

'Philip this is our wedding day,' she shouted. 'How could you do this to me?'

'Glenda darling,' replied Philip, 'I told you only if it was raining. Only if it was raining!'

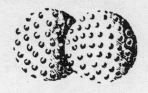

Ron complained his greatest handicap was that he had to play golf with his boss every Tuesday.

An Irishman was invited to play a round of golf and he arrived at the 1st tee without clubs but carrying a cricket bat, a rake and an umbrella.

'Where are your clubs?' asked one of the golfers.

'I use these,' said the Irishman indicating the bat, rake and umbrella.

'Use those?' chorused the other players.

'Why of course,' replied the Irishman. 'Anyone can play with golf clubs but to make the game more difficult I use the bat as a driver, the rake as an iron and the umbrella as a putter — gives you more satisfaction when you win.'

'I suppose it does,' commented one of the players, 'do you do it with anything else?'

'Do it with all physical activities. Play tennis with a frying pan.'

'All physical activities eh? Well now ...'

'Standing up in a hammock.'

Poor Golfer: 'Well how do you like my game?'
Good Golfer: 'Very good but I still prefer golf.'

The doctor tapped his fingers as he looked at his patient, 'If I were you I'd play a round of golf every day for my health.'

'But I do play a round of golf every day,' replied the patient.

'In that case I'd give it up.'

Bob Hope tells of the time he was challenged to a round of golf by the blind golfer, Charlie Boswell.

'Sure I'll play with you,' said Hope. 'And if you like we can have a small bet.'

'50 dollars?'

'Okay,' replied Hope. 'What time do we tee off?'

'Two o'clock in the morning.'

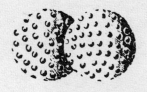

Jimmy Tarbuck claims that when he putts well he is a good putter but when Michael Parkinson putts well he has a good putter.

Alan and his wife Sandra were playing in County Dublin and Alan, a very keen but unsuccessful golfer, sliced his drive into the woods. As he kicked around muttering to himself he came across a little fellow about four feet high and dressed in green.

Alan looked at the little figure and asked, 'Are you a leprechaun?'

'Shure, that I am,' came the reply.

'Can you grant wishes?'

'That I can.'

'Well I always wanted to be a scratch golfer, can you help?'

'If you are prepared to let your wife spend one hour with me in the woods I'll grant your wish.'

Alan went and spoke to his wife who entered the woods and spent the agreed time. After an enjoyable hour the little chap asked, 'How old is your husband?'

'Thirty-seven,' smiled Sandra.

'And he still believes in leprechauns?'

The young golfer joined an elderly player and asked, 'Why are you looking so sad?'

'Well, young fellow,' said the older man, 'Now that I'm wealthy enough to afford lost balls I can't hit them far enough to lose them.'

'A very successful, but unpopular golfer hit a bad patch and was playing very badly in The British Open Championship. His putting at the third hole was terrible and as he handed his putter to his caddie growled, 'It's a bloody funny game!'

'Yes sir,' replied the caddie, 'but it was never meant to be.'

He arrived at his golf club late. 'It was really a toss up whether I should come here or go to the office,' he explained. Then he added thoughtfully, 'As a matter of fact I had to toss up eleven times.'

Peter lived for his golf, he was generally accepted as being the most enthusiastic player. One evening he arrived home very late and was greeted by his wife, 'Oh Peter I was so worried about Peter Jun. He was away all day but he tells me he caddied for you.'

'Well do you know,' replied Peter, 'he's probably right. I thought I'd seen that boy somewhere before.'

Husband: 'Did I tell you of the fright I got on the golf course yesterday?'

Wife: 'No you didn't tell me but I saw you with her.'

She took a hefty swing and lifted a foot long divot out of the turf.

'What will I do with this?' asked the lady holding up the divot.

'Why not take it home and practice on it,' replied the professional.

First Caddie: 'I believe you're not allowed to caddy for the lady members any more.'

Second Caddie: 'That's right I couldn't learn not to laugh.'

Angus walked into the clubhouse and was immediately stopped by a friend. 'Angus what happened? Your tongue and nose are green.'

'I spilled a wee drop of whisky on the sixteenth green.'

Then there was the golfer who spent the week on a new approach only to discover his wife wasn't going away for the weekend.

An Irishman was about to tee off at the Royal Dublin when a leprechaun appeared beside him and said, 'Would you like to win the British and the Irish Open Championships?'

'Shure now and I'd love to.'

'Would you give up your sex life for a year for it?'

'To be shure,' replied the Irishman.

After the year the leprechaun was again beside the golfer as he was about to tee off.

'How did it feel to be a champion?'

'Wonderful.'

'Did you mind giving up your sex life.'

'Not at all.'

'How often did you have sex before we made our deal?'

'Five or six times a year,' replied the golfer.

'That's not very much!'

'Well, it's not too bad for an Irish priest with a small parish.'

The doctor was talking on the telephone to his golfing partner. 'Yesterday was a terrible day I lost four balls.'

Just then a man in the waiting room who overheard him got up and left quickly.

'Who was that?' asked the doctor as he cradled the receiver.

'Someone called Milliken,' answered the receptionist. 'He wanted to speak to you about a vasectomy!'

Charles: 'The club fined me for hitting my wife with a number nine iron.'

Roger: 'For ungentlemanly behaviour?'
Charles: 'No, for using the wrong club.'

'My wife says if I don't give up golf she'll leave me.'
  'That's terrible.'
  'Indeed, I'll really miss her.'

Lady Golfer: 'That's the twelfth time I've swung at
  the ball.'
Professional: 'Keep swinging. I think you've got it
  worried.'

Beginner: 'What do you think is the most difficult
  thing for a beginner to learn about golf?'
Professional: 'To keep from talking about it all the
  time.'

Gerry took his girl friend Linda for her first game of golf. 'You know what you're supposed to do?' he asked.

'Yes,' nodded Linda. 'Get the ball into the hole.'

'Right, go ahead.'

Linda swung at the ball and got a hole in one.

Gerry was quiet as he took 5. 'There you are,' as he placed the ball on the tee. 'Again.'

Once again Linda swung and the ball landed on the green to roll very slowly and disappear into the hole.

'Gosh,' said Linda, 'I thought I had missed it that time.'

'I'm going to have my son act as my caddie to-morrow.'

'What age is he?'

'Four.'

'He's too young to carry your bag.'

'He's also too young to count over eight.'

After playing a very poor game the unhappy golfer

asked what he should give his caddie. The other golfer shrugged, 'Have you ever thought of giving him your clubs?'

Stan: 'I gave up fishing for golf – and I must say I like golf much better.'

Lawerence: 'Oh you prefer to battle against your fellow man rather than a fish.'

Stan: 'No not really, when you lie about golf you don't have to produce evidence of your expertise.'

Madge: 'We must be getting near the clubhouse.'

Midge: 'Indeed we seem to be running over more golfers with the cart!'

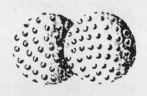

Tom: 'How did you do to-day?'

Jack: 'Great! I shot 9 on the 1st hole, 13 on the 2nd, 15 on the 3rd, but then I made a mess of it on 4th!'

In life as in rugby a try counts but in golf nothing counts like your opponent.

Four men who met every Sunday for a round told how they each managed to get away from his wife every week.

'Well I drop a sleeping pill into her late night cup of chocolate on Saturday night and she sleeps until I get home. Never even misses me.'

'I just say, "I'm going to play golf whether you like it or not!" ' snorted the second.

'I told her I played because of doctor's orders,' said the third.

'Well. I just set the alarm for 6.30 a.m. I nudge my wife awake and I say, Darling, what'll it be, intercourse or golf course?'

The golfer was having a really terrible time and eventually turned to his caddie and snarled, 'This is the toughest course I've ever played.'

'How do you know sir? You haven't been on it yet.'

'Heard the terrible news about Teddy Manders?' one man asked his partner as they walked to the first tee.

'No, what happened?'

'He had a great round on Sunday, finished early, drove home and found his wife in bed with another man! Shot them both! Dreadful affair.'

'Could have been worse.'

'What do you mean?'

'If he'd finished early on Saturday, he would have shot me!'

Lady Golfer: 'Caddie, why do you keep looking at your watch?'
Caddie: 'It's not a watch ma'am, it's a compass.'

'How can I cut down on my strokes?'
'Take up painting by numbers.'

Errol Flynn, a low handicap golfer, claimed he had a very pretty girl as his partner one day and when she selected a club, which he thought unsuitable, for a shot, he asked why she took that particular club.

'Darling,' was the reply, 'the colour of the handle just matches my sweater.'

Barney and Basil were having a chat when a funeral passed. In the front car, instead of flowers there were golf clubs and a trolley.

'That's a lovely tribune to a golfer,' said Basil. 'They're going to bury his clubs with him. He must have loved the game!'

'He still does,' replied Barney. 'It's his wife that died. Immediately after the funeral it's back to the golf course!'

'What's your handicap?'
    'I'm too honest.'

Old Smithers had been a member of the golf club for more than fifty years but he had never been seen actually playing the game but was always to be found at the bar. He had been warned by his doctor, who was also a member of the club, that if he didn't immediately stop drinking he would surely kill himself. However Smithers continued his heavy drinking until one day he collapsed at the bar, glass in hand. His doctor, who was about to tee off, was called and rushed into the clubhouse. One look at Smithers and the doctor knew it was all over. He knelt by the man and said, 'I'm sorry but I told you if you didn't stop drinking this would happen.'

'How long have I?' gasped Smithers.

'About three minutes.'

'Is there nothing you can do for me?'

'Well,' said the doctor, rubbing his chin, 'I suppose I could boil you an egg.'

Every Saturday O'Hara and O'Neill played two rounds of golf. Between the rounds they would find a quiet spot to enjoy their packed lunches and as soon as O'Neill unwrapped his sandwiches he would peer to see what was in them then snort, 'Cheese again!' and throw them away.

This happened every week until at last O'Hara said, 'If you don't like cheese tell your wife not to put it in your sandwiches.'

'She doesn't make them, I do,' replied O'Neill.

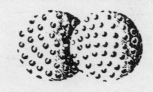

'Coming out for a drink Peter?'

'Not to-day, Davidson is playing in the Ulster Championship.'

'Well what about the weekend?'

'Can't make it, Davidson is playing in the Irish Open.'

'Next week?'

'No, Davidson is playing the British Open.'

'Why the change of game Peter? Your love was always cricket but now you're always watching Davidson playing golf.'

'I don't watch Davidson. When he plays I sleep with his wife.'

Paul: 'What a club this is ... I've never seen such a group of golfers. All have broad shoulders, big hands and thick thighs ...'

Peter: 'Yes and the men are much the same.'

'One more bad shot will drive me crazy.'

'You don't need a drive, – a short putt will do.'

Eric: 'I don't understand you Ron, first you slice the ball into the rough, then into the woods and then you lose it in the river and you still insist on finding it?'

Ron: 'I have to. It's my lucky ball.'

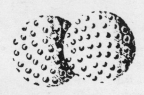

Jack: 'What made your wife take up golf so suddenly?'

Mike: 'Oh, she read in a magazine about somebody finding a diamond in the rough.'

Another Dolly Parton story reveals that when she telephoned to enquire about membership of a golf club the secretary exclaimed, 'Love to have you I'll send you two application forms.'

It is not a sin to play golf on a Sunday but the way some people play it's a crime.

'I just can't figure out how you and your partner beat two world champions and you even had a side bet on. How did you do it?'

'Well you know both those boys have an eye for a beautiful woman.'

'So?'

'My partner was Angie Dickinson.'

The sports shop assistant was somewhat surprised when local 'madam' came in and asked to buy some golf balls.

'This is the best ball we have,' said the assistant. 'If you take this ball we print your name on it free of charge.

'Wonderful,' replied the lady. 'If you print my telephone number on it as well I'll take twelve dozen.'

'I play in the seventies,' quipped Bob Hope.

'When it gets hotter I quit.'

The two girls were obviously new to golf and they were slowly hacking their way around the course much to the annoyance of two male players who were following. The two men didn't want to play through but at the seventh hole when they came upon the two girls kicking around in the long grass they approached and one man asked politely, 'Lost your ball?'

'Oh no,' replied the girl brightly, 'I've lost my club!'

Bing Crosby and Bob Hope were changing in the locker room in preparation for a round when a well known, but who shall be nameless, film producer approached them.

'I bought my wife a new set of clubs to-day,' announced the producer.

'Yeah?' puffed the pipe smoking Bing, 'as a matter of fact I bought my wife three clubs to-day.'

'What,' sneered the producer, 'only three clubs?'

'Yes,' interrupted Bob Hope, 'but they were Beverly Hills, Bel Air and Hollywood.'

A wife suspected that her husband did not play golf as often as he said so she hired a private detective to follow him.

The detective reported back to her that although her husband went to the golf course he did not play golf but did in fact take a lovely young blonde into the nearby woods where they spent the afternoon making love.

'How long do you think this has been going on?' shouted the wife.

'Well,' replied the detective, 'judging by the tan on his backside, I'd say all summer.'

Archie Browne and his wife were playing a leisurely round when, near the 9th, Archie sliced a ball which almost hit a lady golfer who was also playing with her husband.

'I say old man,' shouted the golfer, 'You almost hit my wife.'

'I'm most awfully sorry,' Archie shouted back, 'Do have a shot at mine.'

The two Mexican golfers fought all the way round the course. Practically every stroke caused an argument until Manuel claimed a hole in one on the 17th.

Juan accused him of cheating and Manuel pulled out a gun and shot him.

When the police arrived, Manuel exclaimed, 'Now I really do have a hole in Juan!'

Father Murphy and Father Steele were playing a round one Monday morning after a very busy week-end.

Father Murphy had trouble all the way. At the 14th hole he played into a deep sand trap. Several times he tried to play out but each time the ball rolled back into the hazzard.

After the fifth attempt he stared at the ball his lips tight and his eyes full of frustration. He remained silent for a long time.

'Father Murphy,' said Father Steele, 'that's the most profane silence I've heard!'

'Doctor, my young son got into my golf bag and swallowed all my tees.'

'Well don't panic. I'll send an ambulance immediately. What are you doing in the meantime?'

'I'm practising putting.'

The lady was shocked when she heard young Tommy swearing loudly because he was being beaten at marbles. 'Now, now Tommy,' she admonished, 'do you know what happens to little boys who swear because they are beaten at marbles?'

'Yes they grow up to be golfers,' was the reply.

'Golf is a stupid game!'

'You're absolutely right. I'm glad I don't have to play it again until tomorrow.'

One Sunday morning as he walked to his church the parson met one of his parishioners going to play golf. He pointed an accusing finger at the golfer, 'Come now David you know it's a sin to play golf on a Sunday – but come to think about it the way you play it's a sin any day!'

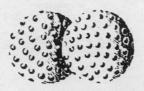

There are three ways to improve your golf: start practising, start lessons, or start cheating.

You always know an English golfer, during business he talks golf and on the golf course he talks business.

She rushed into the lounge and exclaimed, 'Darling I've played my first game of golf.'

Her husband looked interested, 'Wonderful. What did you go round in?'

'Oh my new green trousers, cream polo neck sweater and line sun hat. Really a dream, I was the best dressed girl there!'

Golfers definition of a perfect wife: A beautiful blonde nymphomaniac who owns a pub beside a golf course.

'This is the very devil of a game,' snorted the Irish golfer after missing a very short putt, 'they should either make the hole or the ball bigger.'

'The sporting aspect has gone out of golf,' complained Reggie stalking into the locker room.

'What makes you say that?'

'Well my opponent wouldn't even concede a two foot putt.'

'So what?'

'So it cost me a stroke.'

Doctor: 'What's wrong with the man on the stretcher?'

Nurse: 'He had a golf ball knocked down his throat.'

Doctor: 'Who is the man holding his hand?'

Nurse: 'The golfer who hit the ball.'

Doctor: 'He's showing a lot of concern.'

Nurse: 'Not really, he wants his ball back.'

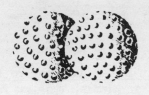

One Sunday morning Charlie was having a terrible time on the course. After one particularly bad shot he exclaimed, 'The way I'm playing to-day, I might just as well have gone to church.'

'I had a wonderful dream last night, I was alone with Angie Dickinson on St. Andrews.'

'Lovely – How did you make out?'

'Great – I went round in sixty-nine!'

Doctor: 'Are you going to take my advice and give up golf?'

Golfer: 'Well if you say I must I will.'

Doctor: 'Well I say you must.'

Golfer: 'Right I'll give it up.'

Doctor: 'Good. Now how much do you want for your clubs?'

After a few drinks a well known television golf commentator admitted, 'It took me twenty years to realize that I know nothing about golf.'

'Why don't you give it up?' asked his fellow drinker.

'I can't – it's too late I've become an authority on the game.'

Golf Duffer: 'How would you have played that shot?'

Golf Professional: 'Under an assumed name.'

Errol Flynn was asked to play in a foursome the following day a 0800hrs.

'Be glad to,' replied the star. 'But if I'm not on time start without me because I'll only be three minute late.'

'Will do,' replied one of the golfers.

'Oh, another thing,' continued the actor. 'Do you mind if I play right or left handed?'

'Not at all,' said the golfer. 'But don't you know how you play?'

'Not until to-morrow morning. If my wife is lying on her right side I play right handed, if she's lying on her left side I play left handed.'

'What if she's lying on her back?'

'That's when I'll be three minutes late!'

ADVERTISEMENT IN LOCAL NEWSPAPER.

For sale. Husband's set of golf clubs and trolley.

Original price £250. Will accept £20. Telephone 56983. If a man answers hang up!

'This course,' moaned one golfer, 'has more dog-legs than Cruft's Dog Show!'

It is reported that when ex-President Amin was asked how he, a non-golfer, could hit a ball so far he replied, 'It's easy man, the ball is white!'

'I suppose you've seen worse golfers in your time, caddie?'

The caddie did not reply.

'I said, I suppose you've seen worse golfers in your time?'

'I heard you the first time. I'm just trying to remember.'

'Caddie can I carry that bunker?'
    'I wouldn't think so sir. There's too much sand in it.'

She was very pretty and he was shooting her a strong line of how good a golfer he was. She didn't play golf so he said he would teach her.

The following day at the first tee he prepared to give her a demonstration of how to drive. Taking his driver he swung hard and missed. His second attempt was just as bad and he also missed his third swing.

'Darling,' she said, 'I see that golf is a great game and it's lovely out here but what's the little white ball for?'

Dear Sir,
I must advise you that you cannot deduct golfing equipment as medical expenses.
Yours faithfully,
I. Takem.
Tax Collector.

Dear Tax Collector,
The way I play makes me sick.
Yours faithfully,
I.B. Ailing.

Richard came across two women searching in the rough. 'Trouble?' he asked.

'I've lost may ball,' replied the first lady golfer.

'What sort of ball was it?' enquired Richard.

'A brand new one – never been properly hit yet!' cut in the second lady golfer.

He tried hard but his golf got worse until one day it took him over six hours to get round the course. Even he knew it had to be rather long and he thought he should make it up to his caddie.

'What do you think I should give the caddie?' he asked the club professional.

'How about your clubs, sir?'

O'Hara was having trouble with his game. He was losing distance off the tee and was having to use two more irons to reach the green. As his game got worse he went to a doctor who was also a golfer.

After an examination the doctor said, 'Well I know why your game is going off.'

'Well there's good news and bad news. What do you want first?'

'The bad news.'

'The reason that you're playing so badly is that you're undergoing a sex change — you'll soon be a woman!'

'And the good news?'

'You'll be able to play off the ladies' tee.'

Wilson was mad about golf. It was his only topic of conversation. Mrs. Wilson was being driven insane by the constant talk of birdies, sand-traps, courses and greens.

Finally, as they were going out one night she snapped, 'I'm fed up with your talk of golf. That's all you can talk about golf – golf – golf! It don't want to hear another word about golf.'

'But what will we talk about then?'

'About anything except golf. Talk about sex for a change.'

'OK,' said Wilson. 'I wonder who my caddie is sleeping with these days?'

Frank Sinatra claims that Dean Martin loves golf because he can start out with a golf ball and end up with a high-ball.

When a wife brings home information from the golf club, it's gossip.

When a husband does likewise, it's news.

'I wouldn't say you were the worst golfer I've ever seen on this course, but then madam,' added the caddie, 'I've seen places to-day I've seen before!'

In the mixed foursome the man gave his partner a terrible telling off.

'You're the worst player I've ever seen. You shouldn't be allowed on a golf course. A three month old baby could do better!'

On the other side was a charming lady.

'Excuse me,' she said as she walked with the other woman to the clubhouse, 'but I couldn't help overhearing your husband shouting at you. I thought he was very cruel.'

'He's not my husband,' said the woman. 'I just live with him. You don't think I'd marry a swine that!'

Shaun O'Hara wanted to improve his drive so after his shot he would grab his tee and run backwards so he could add ten yards to his drive.

The only reason he was a scratch golfer was that his dog had fleas.

'It was my wife who drove me to golf,' admitted John Player, 'and you know I never even thanked her for it.'

Many a golfer would rather have a golf cart than a caddie as it cannot count, cough, criticise or chuckle.

Funny game golf. It always seems that the slowest people on earth are those in front of you whilst the fastest are those behind.

'What made you change the date of your wedding?'

'Well I reckoned if I didn't my silver wedding anniversary would fall on a Sunday and I always play golf on a Sunday.'

Many a husband has a secret craving to use his golf clubs in a way the maker never intended.

When Father O'Kane accepted the challenge of Ronald Drew, the atheist, the Roman Catholic Church showed a great interest, particularly as Drew had promised he would give £1000 to charity if he lost.

Both men were experienced golfers but Father O'Kane had a two stroke lead when they reached the 17th green. He had to sink a five foot putt and, as he had done before playing every stroke, closed his eyes and prayed. He played the shot and the ball rolled about two inches passed the hole and as it did so the heavens shook as a great voice boomed out, 'Dammit, I missed!'

Husband: 'Darling, I have a present for the person I love most in all the world.'
Wife: 'A set of golf clubs no doubt.'

Jane took her tenth swipe at the ball, 'Thank goodness it's gone at last!'

The caddie shook his head, 'It isn't the ball that's gone miss – it's your charm bracelet!'

Ian seated himself at the breakfast table and said, 'Really looks a beautiful day.'

'Well you needn't think you're going to play golf,' said his wife, 'there are too many jobs to be done around the house.'

'Golf was the furthest thing from my mind,' protested Ian. 'Now would you please pass the putter?'

The pretty young girl asked to see the secretary of a very exclusive golf club in Kent. An interview was arranged and the secretary was shocked when the girl told him she was pregnant and the club's assistant professional was responsible.

'What?' exclaimed the secretary. 'Our assistant! Think of the club. The scandal.'

'Think of me,' replied the girl. 'Something will have to be done this time.'

'Of course, of course,' the secretary paused for a moment then asked. 'This time?'

'Oh yes I already have one child to him.'

'This is outrageous!' thundered the secretary. 'He'll marry you or be sacked!'

'I don't want to marry him,' said the girl. 'I just want a settlement.'

'Why will you not marry him?'

'I don't fancy him!'

'Your husband seems to be hitting the ball better with that new stance.'

'Old stance. New husband.'

A golfer who stuttered was looking for a partner for a round of golf.

The assistant professional suggested he ask the girl on the putting green as she also stuttered.

The man approached the girl, 'Would you care to partner me? I'm Pee ... Pee ... Pee ... Peter, but I'm not a saint!'

The girl smiled and replied, 'I'd love to but I'm not a vir ... vir ... vir very good player!'

Mary O'Neill admitted that when her husband went out to play golf he was usually as fit as a fiddle but when he came home he was as tight as a drum.

Arnold was sitting at the club bar crying softly into his drink.

'Something wrong?' asked the barman.

'My wife ran off with my golfing companion,' sobbed Arnold.

'You'll soon replace her,' said the barman helpfully.

'Yes, but not him,' said Arnold. 'He's the only one in the club I could beat.'

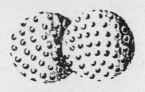

W.C. Fields was addressing the ball at the ladies' tee when another player walked up to him and said, 'Excuse me, but you should be playing off the mens' tee back there!'

Fields gave the man a baleful look and rumbled, 'Not that it's any of your business but this is my third shot!'

As Jimmy Tarbuck once remarked, 'There's nothing so wonderful about a long ball hitter. The woods are full of them.'

When accused of lying the club bore shouted, 'I'm not a liar. I just remember big.'

'You're the club professional so tell me what to do about my game.'

'Well first you should relax and give it up for about six months …'

'And then?'

'Give it up altogether!'

The way some Sunday golfers play they would be better off in church.

Father Murphy was hacking away trying to get out of a sand trap. He finally lifted it out after seven strokes only to land it in another sand trap. He tapped the ground gently with his club as he said through clenched teeth to his companion. 'As a lay man would you say a few appropriate words for me?'

The Irishmen were taking a short cut across a golf course. As the yell 'Fore' was heard the ball struck one man on the head and knocked him to the ground. As he tried to rise his friend pushed him down with the warning, 'Stay where you are there are three more to come!'

A golfer is a man who hires someone to cut the grass, so he can play golf for the exercise.

You know your golf is improving when you can get out of the rough by the same number of shots it took you to get in.

Ken: 'Charles is teaching me to play golf.'
Tom: 'He's a conceited big-head.'
Ken: 'Certainly is. I felt like killing him to-day.'
Tom: 'Why didn't you?'
Ken: 'I didn't know which club to use!'

Harry had promised to partner his wife in a mixed foursome. She had done everything wrong but Harry had forced a smile at all her mistakes. At the last green Harry had played to within one foot of the hole.

His wife giggled, 'If I get this putt I'll drop dead.'

'Promises, promises, promises,' muttered Harry.

The four drunks were playing at Coleraine when one slipped and fell into the River Bann. As he went under for the third time he frantically waved his hand. His three companions watch him then one remarked, 'I think he wants his 5 iron!'

A golfing businessman is one who can carry twenty-five pounds of equipment but needs his secretary to bring him a file.

'Pity about Bert's funeral.'
  'What happened?'
  'They buried him on a hillside.'
  'So?'
  'Bert never did like a downhill lie.'

'I love golf,' said Murphy. 'I'd like to play thirty-six holes every day.'

'You sound really keen,' said his neighbour. 'What's your handicap?'

'My wife,' moaned Murphy. 'She won't let me play at all.'

'How long have you been playing golf?' the club professional asked the new Irish member.

'Oh a couple of months,' was the reply.

'Well you certainly play a very good game.'

'I ought to,' said the Irishman. 'It took me eight years to learn.'

New Golfer: 'I want to be a golfer in worst way.'
Caddie: 'You've already made it sir!'

The vicar, not the best of golfers, was as usual, without a partner, so he approached a new member who said he scored in the high nineties.

As they set out the new member suggested they play for more money than the vicar was used to. The vicar, not wishing to be considered a bad sport, agreed.

However, when they began to play it became very clear that the new member was a much better player than he had claimed and soundly beat the vicar.

'Tell me,' said the vicar, 'do your parents live in these parts?'

'Yes. Why?'

'Well if you bring them round to the church some day I'll marry them!'

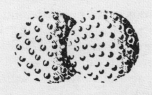

Two members standing at the clubhouse window were watching a lady golfer select a club for third shot to the last green.

'Look at that woman using a wood for a shot like that! The last player who did that broke our ... DUCK!!'

The lady rushed up to the club professional and gasped, 'You're right Tony, my golf is improving. I've just hit a ball in one!

A good golfer hits a ball hard, straight and not too often.

A very famous Hollywood blonde was very attracted to a golf professional and went with him to an important tournament. Her boyfriend's first shot was poor and ended in a sand bunker. His mood was made much worse when his opponent got a hole in one.

'Don't worry darling,' whispered the blonde, 'he'll have a terrible time playing it out of that!'

Notice at a golf club in Scotland:
 'At this club balls are not lost until they've stopped rolling.'

The golfer strode into the long grass to find his ball. He stopped suddenly and politely removed his cap. 'Oh I'm so sorry but please don't move, I'll try a number 5 iron!'

The Chief Officer for Northern Ireland Fire Brigade has an aversion to being called by his rank when engaged in his favourite sport – golf. On the golf course he likes to be called George. One day as he was trying to figure a way out of a sand bunker another golfer called to him, 'Morning Chief Officer.' The Chief Officer shouted back gruffly, 'Good morning to you seller of dresses, brassieres and knickers.'

The golfer's shot was terrible and he sliced the ball to a main road where it hit a bus driver knocking him unconscious. The bus crashed into another bus and they both overturned and soon the air was filled with cries of pain.

The golfer dropped his club threw his hands in the air with a cry of, 'My God, what will I do?'

'You'll have to change your grip,' said his companion. The back of your hand is too far round.'

The two priests had a meeting with the bishop which lasted much longer than they had hoped and as they walked to the car Father Murphy remarked, 'I had hoped the meeting would have been much shorter and we could have had a round of golf before returning to the parish.'

'Well we still can have a round,' replied Father Donal.

'We won't have time, we have to hear confessions in an hour.'

'Who will know?' asked Father Donal. 'They'll just think we were late back from the meeting.'

So it was agreed and the two priests went to play golf.

Father Murphy's first shot was a beauty and he had a hole in one.

However, instead of being delighted he looked

sadly at Father Donal and said, 'The first time I've ever had a hole in one and who can I tell?'

Rich Golfer: 'Caddie are you keeping my score?'
Caddie: 'No sir I didn't bring my calculator with me.'

Howard Thompson, captain of The Northern Ireland Civil Service Golf Team glared at his players who had just lost The Ulster Amateur Cup, 'I've never seen worse driving since my mother-in-law tried to reverse her car into the garage.'

Another Parkinson/Tarbuck story. At a recent Stars' Charity Golf Tournament Michael Parkinson and Jimmy Tarbuck were partners. At the fourth hole Michael Parkinson missed a short putt and waving his putter in the air growled, 'I'm my own worst enemy.'

'Not while I'm your partner,' retorted Jimmy Tarbuck.

The lady golfer had to make a two inch putt but she examined the ground carefully, played a couple of practice swings before playing the ball into the hole. Gleefully she picked the ball out of the cup and turned to the professional, 'Well how many did I take?'

'Seventy-one.'

'Isn't that wonderful?'

'Wonderful,' replied the professional wearily, 'now let's try the second hole.'

An Irishman and a Jew were playing a twosome. After the first hole the Irishman asked, 'How many did you take?'

'Eight,' replied the Jew.

'Ah, I only took seven so its my hole,' said the Irishman.

After the second hole the Irishman again asked, 'How many did you take?'

The Jew smiled knowingly. 'No, no, its my turn to ask first.'

Jimmy Tarbuck was hard at work on a script when Michael Parkinson telephoned and asked him if he was busy.

'Busy!' exclaimed Jimmy Tarbuck. 'Just now my time is worth ten pounds a minute.'

'Well,' replied Michael Parkinson, 'I was going to suggest that you come out with me this afternoon and play about eighteen hundred pounds worth of golf!'

Mrs. Margaret Thatcher was playing very badly and at the last hole exclaimed, 'Dear, dear, there cannot be worse players than myself.'

'Well there may be worse players,' said the caddie indulging in a Thatcherism, 'but they don't play.'

Peters staggered into the clubhouse clutching at his blood covered head.

'Sit here,' said his friend guiding him to a chair, 'and I'll get the first aid kit. What happened?'

'It was at the 16th hole,' groaned Peters, 'I hit a brand new ball out of bounds and couldn't find it anywhere. Saw a cow standing there so I lifted its tail and believe it or not there was a ball stuck there but it wasn't mine, it was a number 4. Just then this woman came along looking for her ball. I lifted the cow's tail and said to her, 'Does this look like yours?' and she hit me with her 3 iron!

As one golfer's wife remarked, 'My husband is the most popular man in the club because they let him have more shots at the ball than anyone else.'

Members of the church have an additional handicap when they play golf – they haven't the vocabulary for it.

To take up golf you must have an open mind – or better still a hole in your head.

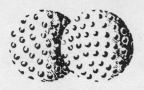

Scots Golfer: 'Caddie can you find balls in the rough?'
Caddie: 'Oh yes sir.'
Scots Golfer: Good, find one and we'll get started.'

When asked what his golf handicap was Harold replied, 'Just that I can't play very well.'

The two men played a round of golf in the morning and then after a purely liquid lunch started on another round each armed with a hip flask. At the fifth hole one asked the other, 'I say old chap do you know how we stand?'

'With great difficulty,' came the reply.

The 19th hole is sometimes referred to as the alco-hole.

The American minister was playing golf and playing it very badly. Every time he played a bad shot he would snort 'Boulder!'. Eventually his opponent asked, 'Why do you keep saying Boulder?'

'Because,' answered the minister, 'it's the biggest dam I know!'

'Why don't you address the ball?' asked the golf professional to the hopeless pupil.

'I will as soon as those ladies move away,' was the grim reply.

Golfer: 'You must be the worst caddie in the world.'
Caddie: 'I doubt it sir.'
Golfer: 'Why?'
Caddie: 'Too much of a coincidence.'

As often happens the caddie knew much more about the game than the golfer and he kept giving advice. Finally the golfer could stand it no longer. 'Shut up,' he yelled. 'I was playing this game before you were born.'

'And I'm trying to get you to finish it before I die,' retorted the caddie.

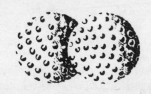

A scratch player handed in his card and the secretary looked at it in surprise, 'Ninety-six! What happened to you to-day?'

'It was that new hazard on the course kept taking my eye off the ball.'

'What new hazard?'

'Angie Dickinson!'

Both golfers hooked their drives into a wooded area. They searched without success. As they searched they were watched by an elderly silver haired lady. Eventually the two golfers gave up and the lady approached them with the question, 'Would it be cheating if I told you where they are?'

Margaret: 'I cut seven shots off my score to-day.'
Mary: 'Wonderful how?'
Margaret: 'Easy. I didn't play the last hole.'

Voice from the woods, 'Caddie never mind looking for the ball, try and find me!'

No matter how you slice it, a golf ball is still a golf ball.

There is a story of Bob Hope who, during a tour of Vietnam to entertain the troops, had a round of golf one day and his caddie was a soldier who knew nothing of golf. Bob Hope had sliced the ball and was studying the lie.

'Well son,' he said to his caddie, 'What do you think I can get home with from here?'

'Gee Mr. Hope,' replied the soldier, 'I don't even know where you live!'

Did you hear about the golfer who had a five footer on the practice green and his wife sued for divorce?

And then there was the absent minded dentist who, about to putt, stared at the hole and said, 'A little wider please.'

The nice thing about golf is that it gives you something to lie about as well as your job.

Golfer: 'Watch my swing, I don't think I'm playing my usual game.'
Professional: 'What game is that, sir?'

Rich American tourist at Royal Portrush Golf Club, 'I don't think I need a caddie.'

Young Irishman: 'I know the course well.'
American: 'Can you count?'
Young Irishman: 'Yes sir.'
American: 'Well add 4, 5 and 3.'
Young Irishman: 'Nine sir.'
American: 'You're hired!'

'Why do you play golf?'
    'To aggravate myself.'

A straight line is the shortest distance between two putts.

He was a very bad golfer and was swinging away at the golf ball which had landed on an ant hill. He

123

whacked until there were only two ants left on the hill along with the ball.

'You know,' said one ant to the other, 'if we're going to survive we better get on the ball.'

He wasn't the best golfer in the world and when he got to the pond hole he hit the ball straight in, with quite a splash. So he unwrapped another ball and mis-hit it into the water as well. He repeated this procedure until he had lost seven new balls in the water.

'Why don't you try an old ball,' suggested his partner.

'Hell dammit!' exploded the golfer. 'I've never had an old ball.'

A recent survey carried out that the worst mathematicians are to be found on golf courses.

The Californian was playing at Royal Portrush in Northern Ireland and was finding the day rather cold.

'Very cold to-day,' he said to his caddie.

'Oh it's not too bad,' answered the man, 'but it can get cold in the middle of winter.'

'Do you play all year round?'

'Yes we do.'

'What happens if it snows; do you paint the balls red?'

'No I usually wear an extra pair of trousers.'

Charlie was happily striding along carrying a new set of golf clubs when he met his friend Mike.

'You're looking very happy,' said Mike.

'Yes indeed I got this new set of clubs for my wife,' answered Charlie.

'Boy that's great! I wish I could make a swop like that!'

The pretty young dancer was asked how she enjoyed her first game of golf.

'Oh great,' she said. 'I was down after only three shots at the fifth.'

'Wonderful.'

'It was,' she said. 'But then the secretary ordered us off.'

Doctor: 'You're very run down.'

Patient: 'What do you suggest?'

Doctor: 'Well I would advise that you lay off golf for a while and get a good day in at the office now and then.'

Girl Golfer: 'What do you think of my equipment?'

Man Golfer: 'Wonderful and you can play golf too.'

A wealthy American business man arrived for a round followed by two men, one carrying the clubs and the other carrying a couch.

'What's the idea of having a caddie carrying a couch?' his partner asked.

'Caddie my foot,' exclaimed the business man. 'That's my psychiatrist!'

Rosemary Murray had just won the ladies cup and was being interviewed by a local reporter. When asked her age Rosemary stalled for a moment then muttered, 'Well you might say I'm approaching 40.'

Seeing some raised eyebrows of her companions she continued, 'Well perhaps not so much of an approach as a putt.'

'And a very short putt at that,' loudly whispered one of the ladies.

'More like a hole in one,' said another.

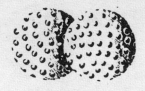

A new television programme is to be screened shortly in which golfers will play snooker players at golf and snooker, it will be called Pot and Putt.

'Jimmy Brown cheats,' said Tom McDowell as he walked into the clubhouse. 'He lost his ball in the rough and played another without losing a stroke.'

'How do you know he didn't find his ball?' asked a colleague.

'Because I've got it in my pocket.'

Ian Davidson and David Renwick, two leading television writers were about to play on a new course when Peter Vincent, another talented writer, said he would like to join them. As Peter was a very poor player they tried to stall him by telling him how tough the course was. But Peter insisted.

Ian and David teed off, each driving his ball about 200 yards. Peter teed up, swing missed! Swing missed! Swing missed! Eventually he hit the ball and it rolled about 4 yards.

'You know,' said Peter, 'you chaps were right. This is a tough course!'

'What's your handicap?'
'My wife.'

For Cyril Smith to play golf would be like a pilot flying blind.

The four ladies were changing in the locker room of the golf club when a hooded male streaker ran in past them then ran out.
First lady: 'Disgusting! I wonder who it was?'
Second lady: 'Certainly wasn't my husband.'
Third lady: 'Nor mine.'
Fourth lady: 'He isn't even a member of the club.'

First Lady: 'I'm a golf widow.'
Second Lady: 'Does your husband play golf all day too?'
First Lady: 'No he was killed at the nineteenth hole when the club house collapsed.'

Golf is the pursuit of pale pills by purple people.

Golf Professional: 'Now the most important thing is to keep your eye on the ball.'
Pupil: 'Oh, so that's the sort of club I've joined!'

Old Golfer: 'I don't know what the club is coming to. Just look at that girl, trousers and short hair. Shouldn't be allowed.'
Partner: 'That happens to be my daughter.'
Old Golfer: 'Oh I'm sorry I didn't know you were her father.'
Partner: 'I'm not. I'm her mother.'

Two Irish caddies were sheltering in a shed during a thunderstorm and the rain came through the roof in all directions. Said one caddie, 'Pat, I'm going out, it'll be drier in the rain!'

Mary: 'Do you like the Aghadowey Golf Course?'
Josie: 'Of course I do. That's where John goes to play bridge.'

'Golf is like marriage. It looks so easy to those who haven't tried it.' – W.C. Fields.

He had always wanted to play golf and play it well so when he won the pools he left his job bought himself the best gear and hired a professional for a month. At the end of the month he had not made much progress and after one particularly poor game

131

confessed, 'I'd move heaven and earth to play this game properly.'

'Well,' smiled the professional, 'you only have heaven to tackle know.'

Roger was surprised when he found out that his golfing partner was having an affair with his wife. However, rather than have an unpleasant scene they decided to play eighteen holes and the winner would have the lady.

'And just to make it interesting,' said Roger, 'let's play for a pound.'

First Wife: 'Does your husband play a lot of golf?'

Second Wife: 'About four times a week.'

First Wife: 'So does mine and now he wants to teach me.'

Second Wife: 'My husband tried to teach me but I still don't know how to hold a tee.'

Frank watched Jack as he was marking his score card. 'I say Jack I don't like the way you cheat on your card.'

'Don't know any other way!'

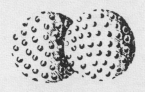

The minister and one of his parishioners had just reached the seventh when some sheep wandered onto the course.

The parishioner was aghast and waved his club in the air yelled loudly, 'Clear off you bastards, clear off or I'll thump you!'

The minister coughed quietly and shook a reproving finger at the golfer. 'Now, now, Cecil, mustn't shout like that at God's creatures. Just say 'shoo shoo' gently and the bastards will clear off themselves.'

After being struck on the head by a golf ball, an outraged golfer charged up to the offender and cried, 'You fool, you hit me, I'll sue you for £5,000.

'I said fore.'

'Alright, I'll sue you for £4000.'

'This is the worst course I've every played on,' snorted the golfer.

'Oh you've played before then?' asked his partner.

Having hooked wildly and killed a hen, the flustered golfer was apologising to the farmer.

'I'm very sorry for killing your hen. Can I replace her?'

'I don't know,' snorted the farmer. 'How many eggs do you lay a day?'

The golfing businessman usually follows his schedule to a tee.

A not so well known golf club in Scotland advertised free golf, free clubs and low accommodation rates provided you purchased the golf balls from the club at £50 each.

'Are you a caddie?'
    'No sir I'm a tea-boy.'

'Shall we play again next Saturday?'
    'Well I was going to get married on Saturday but I suppose it could wait.'

Did you hear about the Irishman who could hit a golf ball 350 yards every time?

It was arranged that he should play the club professional for a prize of £50.

The first hole was par five and the Irishman was

true to form and soared up the fairway. His second shot was also a whopper and landed on the green about two yards from the flag. And his third shot? Once again true to form he hit it 350 yards!

A very keen golfer wasn't feeling well so he went to see his doctor. The doctor told him he was suffering from extreme exhaustion and would have stop playing golf for a year. The golfer, rather annoyed, went for a second opinion and was once again told to stop playing for a year. However, he refused to be daunted and went to a third doctor and was told he could play eighteen holes any time he wanted. The golfer was thrilled.

'Thank you doctor. For that I'll remember you in my will.'

'In that case,' said the doctor, 'play thirty-six holes a day!'

The little man was trying to push his way through the line of golfers waiting to tee off on a new course. The golfers roughly pushed him back. After his third unsuccessful attempt to get through the little man yelled, 'If you push me again I won't open the course!'

'Members of the jury, the Crown can prove that this man killed his wife with malice aforethought.'

'No I didn't,' interrupted the defendant, 'I used a putter.'

A professional golfer noticed a man who turned up at every major tournament. He was always there, hail, rain or shine.

'You must be a very keen golfer,' said the golfer to him one day.

'No,' said the man.

'Are you a photographer?'

'No.'

'A sportswriter?'

'No. Confidentially I'm a pickpocket.'

A reporter from a local newspaper was interviewing Jack Nicklaus.

'According to reports Mr. Nicklaus you made more money last year playing the tournaments than the President.'

'I should,' replied the golfer, 'I play a lot better than he does.'

In Golfers Anonymous when you get the urge to play they send someone over to drink with you until the urge passes.

There is a popular story of a kidnapping attempt on Frank Sinatra which was foiled by a very keen golfer. The famous star asked the man what he would like as a reward and was told a matched set of golf clubs.

A month passed and the man received a telegram from the singer: HAVE YOUR FOURTEEN CLUBS BUT NOT ALL MATCHED STOP FIVE HAVEN'T SWIMMING POOLS.

Ken was disenchanted. 'I wear Jack Nicklaus shoes, Jack Nicklaus shirts, I use Jack Nicklaus clubs, I play the Jack Nicklaus ball ... about as well as St. Nicholas!'

Pity the poor golf professional who was sacked because his work wasn't up to par.

'I didn't know this was a mixed foursome.'
　'It isn't. This is my brother but he has a problem.'

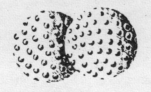

Wife. 'Did you win to-day dear?'
Husband: 'Don't be silly darling, I was playing the boss.'

After spending an hour on the driving range the eager girl golfer asked the club professional 'Do you think I look any better to-day.'

'Very much so. You've changed your hairstyle.'

Judge: 'You have been found not guilty of stealing a set of golf clubs.'

Pat: 'Thank you sor. Does that mean I can keep them?'

First American Wife: 'Did you visit the Holy Land when you were abroad?'

Second American Wife: 'I didn't but my husband did, he said he wouldn't come until he'd been to St. Andrews.'

Pat: 'Tough course?'
Mick: 'Shure is I lost four balls before I teed off!'

Life is like a game of golf. As soon as you get out of one hole you start heading for another.

The Futura Library of Comic Speeches

COMIC SPEECHES FOR SPORTSMEN

For all but the most extrovert, speech-making is an occasion to dread. How do you start? What do you say? What do you do if they don't laugh? Is the cracker of a joke you heard down the pub suitable for the local WI?

THE FUTURA LIBRARY OF COMIC SPEECHES is a new series designed to give you the essentials of a successful, funny speech. Here is all you need to structure a talk, advice on delivery and timing, and a wealth of anecdotes, jokes, shaggy dog stories and strange facts, all geared to the particular audience you're addressing – in this case the world of Sport.

Entertain your audience – and enjoy yourself with THE FUTURA LIBRARY OF COMIC SPEECHES.

FUTURA PUBLICATIONS
HUMOUR

ISBN 0–7088–2985–6

THE BOOK OF EXCUSES

Gyles Brandreth

A COMPLETE GUIDE TO HOW TO COME UP WITH THE PERFECT EXCUSE!

Whoever you are – a child who hasn't done his homework, a husband who arrives home later than expected, a secretary who never gets to the office on time, a zookeeper who can't persuade his pandas to breed – you need an excuse.

They don't always need to be elaborate, but they always ought to be convincing – and with Gyles Brandreth's entertaining guidance and his selection of the most amazing real-life excuses ever known – they certainly will be!

From the government spokesman who excused the fact that Britain had been left behind in the race to the moon on the grounds that we led the world in sewage treatment . . .

. . . to the Unigate milkman who told an industrial tribunal that the reason he joined the housewife in her bath was to help her rinse her empties . . .

. . . to an unemployed accountant who, when asked in court whether he had sold a £3 bag of manure for £650, replied: 'Mark-ups are normal in any profession.'

THE BOOK OF EXCUSES MEANS YOU'LL NEVER HAVE TO SAY SORRY AGAIN!

FUTURA PUBLICATIONS
HUMOUR

ISBN 0–7088–2452–8